HOW DO I TALK TO GOD

HOW DO I FIND FAVOR WITH GOD?

ROBERT JOHNSON

Permission: For information on getting permission for reprints and excerpts, contact:

Parenting Connections Publishing Group
2001 Timberloch Place, Suite 500
The Woodlands, TX 77380
info@parentingconnections.net

All scriptures are from the New King James Version of the Bi-ble unless otherwise indicated.
Scriptures taken from the Holy Bible, New International Ver-sion®, NIV®. Copyright © 1973, 1978, 1984, 2011 by Biblica, Inc.™ Used by permission of Zondervan. All rights reserved worldwide. www.zondervan.com The "NIV" and "New Inter-national Version" are trademarks registered in the United States Patent and Trademark Office by Biblica, Inc.®

Robert Johnson

Edited by: Dr. Tyra Hodge

Copyright ©2023 Robert Johnson
I S B N – 979-8-9866295-8-2 **(Paperback)**

I S B N – 979-8-9866295-9-9 **(eBook)**

I S B N - 9798370501920

HOW DO I TALK TO GOD… HOW DO I FIND FAVOR WITH GOD?

Let me tell you a little bit about myself. I am the author of the book, "The End has Already Passed…Why are You Still Here?" ….. A must-read book.

As a young boy growing up in Long Beach, CA, in the late 1940s and 1950s, our family was rock solid Roman Catholic. I went to church every Sunday until I was about 21 years old. I prayed and prayed and prayed all those years, but all our prayers in the Catholic Church were all repetitions. That is the teaching method of the Catholic Church. We were not taught any different, therefore, we did not know any different.

As the years of my life moved on, I reconnected with the church, but the Catholic Church was not what God had in mind for me.

March 8, 1972

I received my spiritual re-birth in the Lord Jesus Christ on March 8, 1972, at 29 years of age. I do not remember the message given by the guest speaker, Lee Carlton, that night. I only know that it moved me to walk to the altar where a great heaviness was removed from me.

On March 9th, I went back to check out the experience I had had the night before. It was like utopia! I felt as if I was lifted up and walking on air. This lasted for about three weeks.

MAY 2, 3, 1972

I was six weeks old in the Lord when I became ill. It was a very dark night, as I lay stricken in my bed from lung problems and complications. I saw total blackness suddenly divided in half from top to bottom! As the blackness folded up for the top half and down for the bottom half of this blackness, it was overtaken by the most beautiful shade of blue sky that I have ever seen. I saw a man wrapped in this beautiful blue sky. He had on a white gown that looked absolutely breath taking with the blue sky that was behind him. In all my years on earth, I have never ever seen the whiteness and brightness, from head to foot, of the gown of Jesus Christ as he came closer and closer to me on my sick bed. The cloak he had on from the top of his shoulders down to the opposite hip as he faced me was the most beautiful shade of red, white, and blue (not the flag blue). This red had the brilliance of velvet... red velvet. It still takes my breath away as I relive it while writing all this down on paper.

I studied and was fixed on the face of Jesus Christ coming out of heaven. As he was getting closer and closer to me, in all of His radiant glory, I was still fixed on his face. When he got about 15 or 20 feet from me, everything vanished from my view; all the beautiful colors, and Jesus. Suddenly, a white dove came into my view. He was approximately six feet away when he turned and looked at me. His face was the full face of a man. His face was identical to the face of the Lord Jesus Christ. I was only a six-week-old new Christian in the Lord, and I was 29 years old at this time.

I experienced the closeness of death at the time of this vision. When you are so sick and it is a big effort to get up as you become weaker and weaker for weeks, months, or years, everything you see every day in your house takes on a 4th dimension by separation from these things that you see and touch every day in your home. Everything looks different to you as you feel this taking place in your mind, but it is all the same as you saw it before the sickness many occasions in my daily life.

SEPTEMBER 19TH, 1974

I was baptized in the Holy Spirit in the same church I was saved. In the church service that night, there was a spectacular move of the Holy Spirit from the time the service started until its end some three or more hours later. There was an altar call. The Holy Spirit was so heavy on me in this very big church, that as I walked from the back of the church where I was sitting to the altar, I got about halfway to the altar, and I instantly went down to the ground. No one had touched me in any way.

I'm sharing all of this with you to show you what works and what does not work in your prayers. Pay attention. when I got reconnected back into the church, I found a whole new way of prayer. So, I left my repetitious prayer life behind and moved forward into a whole new way of prayer. Now I get answers to my prayers, and I have open communication with God.

You must do your part first. Repetitious prayer is not favored by God because it quickly becomes very mechanical, and it loses its effectiveness, and its meaning becomes far removed from your mind. You do not want that to happen when you are trying to communicate with God, and God does not like repetition in prayer. If you are not in the habit of praying or talking to God, first close your mind from all outside interferences and write down on paper what you want to talk to God about.

_____

_____

_____

_____

_____

_____

_____

_____

First, get your mind set right with God. He wants to hear from you. To find favor with God and to receive answers to your prayers, you must first do your part. Every one of us is a Sinner, whether we admit it or not. It does not change the mind of God if we say to ourselves, I am not a Sinner. It only closes the door to our communication with God. You don't want this to happen if you want a favored prayer life with God.

Prepare your mind and heart to a level to ask God to forgive you of all your sins that you have committed during all your lifetime and really mean it with all your mind and heart. This opens the door of communication between you and God. You must do your part first if this is what you really want.

We all should know about the life and death of Jesus Christ, so take a few minutes out and read in your Bible Matthew, Chapter 27 and 28. Feel and be aware of all the suffering and death that Jesus went through for us. He lived and died to save the human race.

The Bible is filled with scripture in both the old and new testaments about Jesus Christ and what he needed to do to save us from our sins and our sinful nature.

God gave mankind a free will to do whatever he chooses to do, good or evil. Take a good look at the world situation today and see what mankind has done to the earth and to each other all these years. Jesus Christ is still the savior of the world for all those who will come to him on this last day of human history.

About prayer, listen to what Jesus has to say in Mark 11: 22, 23 and 24 in the King James version of the Bible.

"… And Jesus answering sayeth unto them, have faith in God! For verily I say unto you that whosoever shall say unto this mountain (this mountain means the mountain of worries and troubles you are carrying in your mind) be thou removed and be thou cast into the sea, and shall not doubt in his heart, but shall believe those things which he say, it shall come to pass; He shall have whatsoever he sayeth therefore, I say unto

you what things soever you desire of when you pray,
believe that you receive them and you shall have
them."

Remember always, "your best investment is in yourself." so take a deep breath and get yourself ready. With your open mind and heart and all this information that I am sharing with you, you can be assured that God hears and answers prayer. Sometimes God does say no, or not now, or yes. So be ready for whatever God will answer you.

You see, accepting Jesus Christ as savior and Redeemer is a win-win situation for everyone, for whatever the outcome of your prayer may be. Keep this in mind as you pray; God can see far enough in your prayer request future to know if it is a good move for you to make. Remember, God knows the end from the very beginning, so he knows what is best for you and your life, always.

God is an exceedingly kind and loving God, and he wants you to have His very best, if you will accept Jesus Christ as your Lord and Savior. It is not that hard to do. There is not very much time left. This is why it is so very important to reach you with as much information as God has given me to share with you, so that you are not left behind to face the world and what is coming very soon in all the countries of the earth.

The following is an extension of the 23rd Psalm. I hope you will consider this outline to become a source of life and comfort to you regardless of your circumstances and surroundings.

23 PSALM

The Lord is my Shepherd
(This is perfect salvation.)

I shall not want
(This is perfect satisfaction.)

He makes me to lie down in green pastures
(Perfect rest)

He leads me in the paths of righteousness
(Perfect guidance)

I will fear no evil
(Perfect protection)

For thou art with me
(That is company at its best)

Thy rod and thy staff, they comfort me
(Perfect comfort)

Thou prepares a table before me in the presence of my enemies
(Perfect provision)

Thou anoints my head with oil
(Perfect consecration)

My cup runs over
(Perfect joy)

Surely goodness and mercy shall follow me all the days of my life
(Perfect care)

And I will dwell in the house of the Lord forever.
(Perfect destiny)

Jesus Christ is the Good Shepherd of Psalm 23 and is best understood in the Gospel of John, Chapter 10.

So, be patient and wait. God knows all about your life from the beginning to the very end.

Let us take a look at your life and see what the Lord has to say about your life through the prophet Jeremiah Chapter 29: 11, 12, 13 and the first half of verse 14. Here it is… Are you ready?

> *"For I know the thoughts that I think toward you, says the Lord, thoughts of peace and not evil, to give you your expected end. Then you shall call upon me and you shall go and pray unto me, and I will harken unto you. And you shall seek me and find me when you shall search for me with all your heart. And I will be found by you, sayeth the Lord."*

So, you see, we must do our part first as I pointed out several times in this book. Clearly, we are now living the last page of human history and I want to assure you that God will reveal himself to you if he has something that he wants you to accomplish that's important in the saving of people souls. What God has in mind for me to do is to write this book, inspired by the Holy Spirit and to write down the spiritual dreams and visions that God has given me over the past 50 years or so for the outreach of saving lost souls.

I will be sharing some more of my spiritual dreams and visions in this book as we move along. Right now, let's talk about healing. You probably know of someone who is sick or who has been healed and maybe you need healing in your own body. I have written down for you some very powerful Bible chapters and verses for you to consider as you're praying to God for your healing or the healing of someone else. Let us take a look at some healing Bible verses from King James version of the Bible. Remember, clear your mind and focus on what you're going to talk to God about. These healing Bible verses are meant to encourage you. Here are a few of them for you to consider, so take a deep breath:

Malachi 4: 2 "…but unto you that fear my name shall the son of righteousness arise with healing in his wings."

Psalms 107: 20 "…he sent his word and healed them and delivered them from their destruction."

Exodus 23: 25 *"…and ye shall serve the Lord your God and he shall bless thy bread and thy water, and He shall take sickness away from the midst of thee."*

These are only a few that I am writing down in case you don't have a Bible with you. I will share more with you later.

Anoint your property, home, vehicle with oil that you have prayed over to ward off all evil forces. I want to share with you another one of my spiritual dreams. Evil forces are real, and they want to hunt you down. The power is in your hands through Jesus Christ our Lord to keep them at bay.

Evil forces are much stronger than you and me, however, they are NOT stronger than Jesus Christ! They are very real, and they can control your mind and body to do whatever they want you to do unless you are covered in the blood of Jesus Christ as your Savior. Look at the world today. All of this is done by evil forces who live in the hearts of men. We will talk more about this later in this book.

MAY 31ST, 2012

Last night as I was asleep in my bed, I had a very disturbing visitation by several evil forces. In this dream, I had moved into a new apartment and everything I had was still all boxed up. I had two little dogs with me. As I was unpacking, I heard a very loud commotion outside down the street, some distance from my new apartment. The noise was so frightening that total fear gripped me within my heart, mind, and soul. I quickly stopped my unpacking and opened the door to see what all the noise was about. Standing in front of me were four evil looking demons who had come up to my open door. They had been the cause of all this terrifying noise down the street and now they were standing at my open door. They started yelling and screaming at me in many blood-curdling voice ranges. I was so terrified; I could not move. Then, one of them yelled out at me, "Turn your television set down! Your neighbors are complaining." Strangely, my television was off. I was pretty shaken up and upset.

Once I was able to regain my composure, I continued to unpack. My two little dogs became hungry, so I went to look for their food. I searched everywhere in my apartment for dog food, but I had none. This meant that I had to go and purchase some. When I opened the door of my apartment, these four same evil creatures were still standing there. They had a very great hatred in their eyes and on their faces towards me. They entered into my apartment again and began screaming so loudly at me, with so much hatred, I thought they were going to kill me. Then, they all suddenly left.

I managed to somehow go to my bed later and sleep. During this same dream, I was in a deep sleep when suddenly, up through the floor came the hands and arms of these evil forces. They extended up to eye level. I was terrified! I sat up quickly in my bed and began crying out, as loud as I could, over and over again "Lord, where are my weapons!" My loud outcries woke me up from this horrific nightmare.

Folks! This is real; hell is real enough for me to want to do everything I can to keep you from sending yourself there. That is why, I am writing this book...to expose these evil forces to you in the very best way that I can. I do not want you to go where your soul burns and you will feel tortured forever. You may ask, "what is the soul?"

This is what the soul is. The soul lives inside your body. It is a spiritual thing not a physical one. When you die, as your body shuts down, you are transformed into one of two places... heaven or hell. Heaven, I have shared with you in this book and in, "The End has Already Passed...Why are You Still Here?"

The five senses are those senses that we all have. Look them up in the dictionary for the absolute best description. Site, hearing, touching are just three, if I remember from my school days. Pain and suffering are at the top of the list. The soul is exactly what your body is and that's from what God has shared with my dreams and visions. I am going to be sharing more of them in this book.

Again, I want to strongly encourage you to purchase the book by Mary Kay Baxter, "A Divine Revelation of Hell." You will walk away a very well-informed person on hell.

The people in hell are constantly being tortured with fire and brimstone. All in all, these five senses live inside the soul. You see the way we breathe here on earth. We breathe in and out without pain and suffering. The constant suffering and immense pain of the souls in hell will be with their every breath, every second for all eternity. I explained what eternity is in detail in my first book. Pick up a copy for yourself and for others and allow Jesus to save you and them from hell.

There is another sense that is not of the five senses. It is the 6th sense. It is called common sense. I have tried to explain to you what the Holy Spirit has told me to say in this book. So, whatever he continues to tell me is what I will write for your own information.

This book is about you and for you. Do the math! It is so simple. In both of my books, I have tried to show you right from wrong, good, and bad, and these visions and spiritual dreams that I have had. I am writing each and every word down in this book as the Holy Spirit gives them to me. Are you doing all the math to sort all this out? The Sixth Sense that we were talking about would have a perfect application in deciding on the Lord Jesus Christ as your savior and Redeemer.

With all these spiritual dreams and visions, it caused me to sit up and take note since some of them are connected to evil forces. And all these many years later, I know that this book you are reading is the start of the last spiritual revival to reach out to all the people in the world on these last days of human history.

If you start reading the Bible and do not know exactly where to start, try starting in the book of John. There is a wealth of information about who Jesus is and what he is all about. This is heavy, so pay attention. We were all born into sin when we came into this world. You don't feel it or know it because you are born with it. The gospels explained this is in much greater detail than what I can in this book. Again, let's start in the gospel of John. We see that the Lord Jesus Is a very loving, merciful, and forgiving God as we read the gospel of John. Put on this mindset and see how Jesus sees you with this great love that he is offering you.

Let's look at John 3: 16-17 and see what they say. If you don't have a Bible, I will write it out for you. John 3: 16-17 are taken out of the King James versions of the Bible.

John 3: 16 reads as follows, *"For God so love the world, that the Holy Father gave his only begotten son, the Lord Jesus Christ, that whosoever believes in him should not perish but will have everlasting life."* This is what we are working for and trying to reach.

Look at John 3: 17 and see what it says, *"From God the Father sent not his son (Jesus Christ) into the world to condemn the world, but that the world might be saved through faith in Jesus Christ."*

So, you see, this is a message for your salvation. The word of God, the word of love, it's all for you and me. The whole book of John is all about love from Jesus Christ for you and me.

What is faith and how do I get it? The Bible tells us that we all have faith, starting out it may be only as small as a grain of mustard seed, which is the very smallest of all the seeds. To exercise what faith you have, check this out and watch your seed of faith grow that you have planted. 2nd Corinthians 9:6, *"He who soweth sparingly, he shall also reap sparingly, but he that soweth bountifully shall also reap bountifully."*

You see we all have choices to make, either good or bad; this is what this book is all about. Jesus Christ is your choice now…today! Pray and read the gospel of John.

Faith is proof that something exists though we do not see it. Take electricity for example. We all see the results of what electricity does for us in our own daily lives. But do we see electricity? Your seed is faith.

1. Your seed must be planted with faith. This is what you're trusting God to help you with or do for you. What have you asked God for in your prayer? Do you have faith that he will answer your prayers? This is faith... it is talking to you.

2. You must let go and turn your seed loose unto God. Remember you must also pray for the other people and keep their needs in your prayers, so that you can have a higher level of faith answered prayer. Read Matthew Chapter 5, the Sermon on the Mount and try the try to follow these guidelines.

3. You must plant your seed in what you expect to harvest. Are you praying for healing in your body or in the bodies of others that are sick?

What about your other family that you have not seen or heard from in a long time? I cannot answer you with God's own personal information. Pray to God right now for your salvation and accept the Lord Jesus Christ as your God. Savior and Redeemer.

4. Your harvest size is established by your faith when your seed is sown. You want to get the highest favor from God that you can for your prayers to be fulfilled. Are you praying for others and their well-being? Have you helped anyone in need lately? Have you accepted the Lord Jesus Christ as your God and savior? See, these are all things that put you in the heart and mind of God. Remember you must do your part first. God is waiting in heaven to hear from you.

5. Your seed must be planted in good ground. Let's look at Matthew chapter 13: 4-30. It is too numerous to write, but it is a very good

investment, especially since you are trying to find the very highest favor level with God.

6. You must always wait a period of time. Remember, seed planting in the ground does not immediately spring up. It takes the early and latter rains in their seasons to grow and be harvested in full. In the meantime, while you are waiting, continue in prayer and reach out to others physically and in prayer so you can have the very best favor for your prayers. This will work for you if you really want it to.

7. You must maintain your crops (prayers) daily for a proper harvest. Keep the weeds out! Keep your doubt out and replace it with your faith. In the crops that are grown for food to feed people, during the months that it takes to grow the seed for food, weeds rise up out of the ground and they have to be killed. Yes, they will rise up out of the ground again shortly after and the weed elimination and start all over again until the

harvest of the crop. If the weeds of the harvest are not kept under control, the whole harvest dies. The very same is with our prayers. The weeds of your prayers are all the evil forces. They are trying to shoot your prayers full of holes. So, guard over your prayers by praying every day and rebuke all the evil forces who are coming up against your prayers. The evil forces that are coming up against you and your prayers have centuries and centuries of experience. Remember, this is very important; "discouragement" is the biggest tool the devil has to use against you and everyone. Remember, *"Greater is He that is in you than he that is in the world."* Jesus is now and always will be greater!

8. A part of your harvest is for sowing again. Be sure to keep other people in your prayers especially the neediest and contact and help people. This is your sowing again harvest.

9. Part of your harvest is for you to keep. It belongs to you. Jesus will lead you in all things so learn to rely on and trust in Him always.

10. Your harvest is a miracle from the Lord so always thank him and look to Jesus for your salvation. These are not the words of man; these are the words of God.

The apostle Paul clearly makes this story of the seeds in the book of Second Corinthians.

These ten guidelines are not a part of written Second Corinthians, but I wrote them down for you to help you understand about the seed and sowing seed and most of all, faith.

What are you now going to do about accepting the Lord Jesus Christ, since now you know so much more about Him? You now know how to find favor with God. It is all about Jesus, it always was, and it always will be. It is now your move.

The evil forces that I have encountered all these years have tried to be a discouragement in reaching you with this book. Yes, the evil forces know the past and future of our lives but not the future of when the rapture of the church will take place. Only God the Father knows the time and day that this will happen.

The evil Satanic forces have left many of you alone because they already have you and because you will not take the words of this book seriously, or you are just not afraid of God. One thing is for sure, my friend, all of your life is going to catch up with you when your time has come to an end, and it is time for you to leave this world.

So, look, here is the deal! Are you going to save yourself or are you just going to throw yourself away and make hell your home and final destiny? Today is the time to decide!

It's not a sign of weakness in accepting the Lord Jesus Christ as your Savior and Redeemer. What is

Redeemer? It is someone who has saved you from something so very terrible that you could not save yourself from. This book tells you how to be saved and you may have to read this book more than once in order to fully grasp on to what you want to do with your life.

First of all, Jesus Christ came down to earth to show us how to live and find favor with God. The Old and New Testaments are full of the guidelines of how to live our lives pleasing to God. Again, you have to take the first step. Jesus died on the cross to save you and me. Go back and look at the passages in this book to be saved and mark these passages with a bookmarker or underline them with a red pen. Make the best decision of your life in accepting the Lord Jesus Christ as your God and Savior. By doing this, as time moves on in your life, you will see that it is the best decision you could have ever made. How about today?

Let's talk about Jesus for a few minutes in the flood, the sin and evil and wickedness from people and what they were doing to each other and the worship of idols and statues for a very long period of time is why God decided to destroy all of his creation with flooded waters. He did exactly that, except for Noah, his wife, and his family. God is a loving God, and he loves you, too. That's why he sent Jesus to be the one and only Savior of the world. He died for you and me and for all people who would accept Jesus Christ as our Lord and Savior.

As this book moves forward, we will be talking more about Jesus Christ and all He has done in our lives and still does today. Yes, it's true that Jesus could have come down from the cross since He is and was all powerful. If He had, all humanity and creation would have been lost. Jesus Christ is deserving of all of our worship and so is God the Father and God the Holy Spirit. Jesus Christ died to save us all. Are you on board yet? Do not wait too long. Remember, we are not promised tomorrow or even our next breath.

The evil forces in Jesus's days are well known in the scriptures in Matthew, Mark, Luke, and John. We can read how Jesus, on many occasions, cast demons out of people's lives. The people standing around could see what was happening so even today, evil forces can make themselves visible in the lives of people if they so choose to. Remember, the evil forces and evil religious leaders who put Jesus to death on the cross and all the suffering he went through at the hands of evil men were all inspired by evil forces. It was such a big prize to put Jesus to death and kill the Jesus movement before it got started. Jesus, the son of God, would be forever in the grave, never to rise ever again. All the evil forces must have been overjoyed. I can only imagine how they must have been celebrating by having a spectacular event for all the other evil forces as well as the evil human beings that put Jesus to death.

But wait! Jesus said, *"In three days I will be raised from the dead and I will be alive forevermore"*, and He was raised, and He is alive forevermore! And the Jesus movement is alive and well and has been for over two thousand years. Millions of people have been saved who their trust and put their faith in Jesus Christ our Savior.

Now, I would like to share good spiritual dreams and visions that the Lord has blessed me with.

This vision came to me some 40 plus years ago. I was very sick back then and close to dying, so I felt as this condition of sickness was real. When you are that sick you are transformed to another dimension in your body and your mind period your possessions and surroundings in your home have a way of separating themselves from you in your overpowered mind.

As I laid sick on my bed in this vision, I felt my lungs depleted from oxygen. I was standing up and suddenly my fingers were super energized with this heavy power. I lifted my hands and fingers up from my sides and looked at them and they look no different than what they usually do. However, the power was so strong in my fingers that I can only describe it as powerful laser beams in all my fingers.

A very old little woman with red hair appeared and stood in front of me, very sick unto death. She was very thin and only about 5 feet tall. She was very pale and had very white skin. She stood before me, as if she was waiting for me to lay my hands on her to be healed. I raised my hands toward her. I looked again at my extremely powerful fingers as I reached out to her to place my fingers on her forehead; but before I did this, a thought raced through my mind of this tremendously awesome power in my fingers.

I withheld my hands from touching her because this impressive power in my fingers were so strong that if I touched her, I was fearful of sending her back into molecules. Yes, the power was that great in my fingers in that vision.

APRIL 8, 2012 (EASTER SUNDAY MORNING)

In this vision, I was in a very large building with about 70 or 80 coworkers. All of us knew each other fairly well. We all followed our regular routine in the workplace. Lunchtime came for all of us at one time. We all walked out of the building through the same door and found ourselves on top of a mountain. The peace and safety that I felt over me was overwhelming. While all the others stood on the mountain top, I was compelled to run quickly and very fast. I ran and ran and ran on this mountaintop until I was completely out of breath. A voice in the air told me to start running again and my lungs were filled with air and the drive was pushing me to keep running. As I did, I was suddenly flying very high over the mountain top and touching the clouds.

I looked down on the mountain top and saw all the coworkers who had come out of the building with me standing and looking up through the sky. I was absolutely amazed to be flying up so high in my body. In this vision, on the next day, I was again flying high over the mountaintop touching the clouds again I looked down on the mountain top and it was covered with lush green grass as if it were a carpet, so thick and ever so beautiful in color just like all the trees and the bushes that were on the mountain top. They were all full of life, very much unlike the day before as I was flying high over the mountain top in this vision and saw only dust and dirt and no life on the mountains.

In this same vision, I flew down to the ground, guided supernaturally. I was standing in water and was so amazed at how easy it was to walk on water.

The reason I am sharing all this information and visions with you in this book is to try to prove to you that God is real, and Jesus really did suffer and die for you and me on the cross. He does not want you to suffer and burn in hell, but only you can put yourself there. Take a look at these Bible verses written with you in mind, Isaiah 54:10, *"...for the mountains shall depart and the hills be removed; But my kindness shall never depart from thee, and neither shall the covenant of your peace be removed, says the Lord."* **Jude 24 and 25,** *"...now unto him that is able to keep your you from falling and to present you faultless before the presence of his glory with exceeding joy, to the only wise God our Lord and savior Jesus Christ be all glory and majesty dominion and power both now and forevermore. Amen and Amen.*

July 4th, 2021

Last night, in this vision that I mentioned before, I dreamed that I had walked on water on a very large lake. In this vision, I was amazed at how easy it was to walk on water! Because this vision is especially important, I saved it for last. Try to place yourself in this situation. It is about the devil and evil forces pulling you into hell.

APRIL 5TH, 2015, (EARLY EASTER SUNDAY MORNING)

In this vision, it was early in the morning hours. As I lay asleep in my bed, the scope of my mind enlarged once again. A friend of mine and I worked in a place similar to a chemical plant. The plant we came upon had a very large pit filled with a very thick liquid. I didn't pay very much attention to it. The consistency of the liquid was very thick and sticky. This friend somehow was in this pit. I heard his desperate cry for help since I was standing next to the pit at the edge. This pit was filled with quicksand, very ugly green and black in color. Three times this ugly green and black quicksand pull this friend down below the surface of the pit. My consciousness snapped within me, and I realized this friend was in serious trouble unto death as he surfaced the third time. I reached my hand down to pull him out of the pit, but the ugly green and black quicksand would not let my friend go. After a very hard struggle back and forth, for what seemed like hours, I finally pulled him out of the pit. My friend was very nearly dead and naked. I quickly covered him up, but he was so weak he could barely walk. We were finally able to walk on and the vision was over.

The evil forces have the same stranglehold as this quicksand, especially at your time of death. You will be pulled down into hell if you have not made the right decision about the Lord Jesus Christ.

I will do my very best in this book to inform you about the truth about heaven and hell. The rest is up to you. Choose Jesus Christ and live with him and us in heaven or choose not to believe in Him and live in hell in torment.

Are you still on the fence? I can only remind you once again. Spend $15 and read the book, "A Divine Revelation of Hell," by Mary Kay Baxter.

If you are not in the habit of praying or talking with God, you may be asking yourself, "How do I talk to God…How do I find favor with God?" First, clear your mind of all outside interference and write down on paper what you want to talk to God about.

_____

_____

_____

_____

_____

_____

_____

_____

_____

_____

_____

_____

_____

_____

Let's get our mind set right with God and ask ourselves what pleases God, what is most important to him? If we take a look at Matthew chapter 5, it is the only time that Jesus spoke to where all the people understood what Jesus was saying to them.

The remainder of the time he spoke only in parables, so His sermon on the mount must have been very important to him and to us.

Look into your own life and see if you are doing any of these things if you don't have a Bible, I will write this out for you.

Matthew Chapter 5 (The Sermon on the Mount)

Blessed are the humble, for theirs is the Kingdom of heaven.
Blessed are they who mourn, for they shall be comforted.
Blessed are the meek, for they shall inherit the earth.
Blessed are they who hunger and thirst for righteousness, for they shall be well satisfied.
Blessed are the merciful for they shall receive mercy.
Blessed are the pure in heart for they shall see God in heaven.

Blessed are the peacemakers for they shall be called the sons and daughters of God.
Blessed are those who are persecuted for the sake of justice for theirs is the Kingdom of heaven.
Blessed are you when men reproach you and persecute you and speak evil against you for my sake.
Be glad and be happy for your reward is great in heaven; For they persecuted the prophets before you.

This Sermon on the Mount is from my copy of the Ancient Eastern text written in 550 AD. These guidelines are very important to God.

It's really possible to get close to God if you really want to. So, on this last page of human history (I estimate between 8-10 years left), it is very important for you to decide where you are going to spend eternity. That is what this book is all about! So, I will be going to and from spiritual dreams and visions that the Lord has given to me to share with you so you will know that God is truly real, and he is still in charge of the world. Just remember, your life could be over as soon as tomorrow!

Back in the late 1940s and 50s when I lived in Long Beach CA, earthquakes were fairly common. They were only a 3.2 to a 3.5, it was only strong enough to rattle the windows and walls and knock a few things off of the shelves onto the floor. We all got used to the earthquakes since there were so many of them and no one got hurt or died.

Earthquakes, tornadoes, and natural disasters are a part of everyday life in many parts of the world, even here in the United States of America. In this vision, the earthquake was far worse than any I had ever lived through physically in the late 40s and 50s.

With pen and paper, I cannot describe the devastation I saw in this vision. Live electrical wires were down all over the place especially all over the streets, so no vehicles or people could pass. On the grass, in safe areas, I traveled in my truck to this other location that I thought would be much safer for me to be in. As I arrived in this other location, I saw much more devastation than what I had seen in the first location that I was in.

Everything was flattened to the ground. Roads, houses, and buildings that once were, were no longer there. Upon arriving at this new location, a man in uniform told me that I should have stayed at the other location where I was at. He told me that since I was now here to go down to this building that was about 50 feet away and for me to stay in there, and I did.

And there must have been a very powerful aftershock because the next thing I knew, I was knocked out and on the ground. I came to at some point and next to me was a 40- or 50-foot section of roof. I was lying on the ground, and I heard a very loud voice saying to me, "Get up! Get up! Get up! Get up off the ground!" Four times I heard this said to me. I looked all around me and not one person was anywhere for as far as I could see through all this earthquake devastation. I woke up from this vision and no one was in my house.

This was a very shaking up experience and I started thinking how great and awesome the power and strength of God is. I don't want to ever be on the anger side of God. What about you? Do you want any of this to come down on you?

Why do people have spiritual dreams and visions? It's to warn people of what is coming on the earth, and it is well on its way right now. All the prophets in both the old and new testaments talked about all this devastation coming on the earth. The Book of Revelation, that many people don't want to read, is your escape route of knowledge to inform yourself and be able to avoid you're sending yourself to a very real hell.

You have a wealth of information in this book…right here, right now. Take another look at the title of this book, "How do I Talk to God… How to Find Favor with God?" Are you serious enough to want this? Jesus is not going to wait on you forever. There is just going to be a point that he might just give up on you. You don't want this to happen! Take a look at your own comfort zone. Is this holding you back? You have friends and family now, but when you die, you're going to walk that lonesome valley alone, right into hell if you don't have the Lord Jesus Christ as your Lord and Savior and Redeemer. How about it? Find a quiet place right now away from everything and everybody and talk to Jesus in your own words.

_____

_____

_____

_____

_____

_____

_____

_____

_____

_____

_____

_____

Tell him you know you are a Sinner. We all are. Ask him to forgive you of all your sins and mean it from your heart, sincerely. A spiritual transformation will take place in your body that you will feel. You will feel such awesome peace and you will also feel weightless because all your sins have been lifted off of you. The feeling that will come over you will be that you want to tell everybody, and you will.

Take this step with me now. Jesus is waiting to hear from you. Talk to him right now in your own words and let him know that you are very sorry for all your sins, and you know that he suffered and died to save you from all your sins. He paid a debt he did not owe. I owed a debt I could not pay. Tell Him you want Him to be your Lord for all your life. It's all up to you, but that's how to do it.

Take a look with me at 2 Chronicles, Chapter 7:14 (Old Testament). If you don't have a Bible, I'll write it down here for you. *"If my people which are called by my name shall humble themselves and pray and seek my face and turn from their ways, then I will hear them from heaven and I will forgive them their sins and heal their land."*

Let's look at another promise in Bible scripture, 1 Corinthians, Chapter 15: 51-54. This scripture has to do with the title of my first book, "The End has Already Passed; Why are you Still Here?" Are you ready? Here we go!

> *"Behold, I show you a mystery; We shall not all sleep, but we shall all be changed. In a moment, in the twinkling of an eye, at the last trump; for the trumpet shall sound and the dead shall be raised up incorruptible and we shall be changed (all God's children). This corruptible must put on incorrupt and this mortal must put on immortality so when this corruptible shall have put on incorruptible and this mortal shall have put on immortality, then shall be brought to pass the saying that is written, death is swallowed up in victory."*

"Oh death, where is thy sting. Oh grave where is thy victory."

I've tried my best in this book to answer questions you may have and to show you the best way to go as we all move on into eternity, heaven, or hell. What's it going to be? Have you talked to Jesus yet? Have you accepted the Lord Jesus Christ as your Savior and God yet? It's almost over. Don't wait too much longer.

I will also be sharing with you more Bible scripture and some words of my own as the pages of this book continues to move forward. My intention for this book is to show you that God can be very real in your life. After all, He and only He is the true author of this book. I am only writing down what he is telling me to write down, in hopes that you will accept the Lord Jesus Christ as your Lord and Savior as so many millions of us have already done.

November 1, 2021

In this vision, I saw a very terrifying heat coming on the earth. This coming heat will be unbearable, and many people and animals will die from it. This heat that we are experiencing today is not anywhere near the heat that's coming in the tribulation. The coming heat, that I saw and felt in this vision, is going to slice through you like a knife. You will feel it burning and cooking you from the inside out and there will be no relief, neither by day nor by night.

Along with all this heat your knees and legs will greatly shake and buckle. If you leave your house, you will say to yourself, "Why did I leave my house?" Along with all of this is, I saw coming a terrifying fear in the air. It will be a much greater fear to be on the outside than there will be on the inside of your house. This heat will be the same heat that came over the two cities in Japan that ended World War II, radiation heat.

A few months later, after the heat vision, another vision came to me and millions more people and animals will be killed. From the sky will fall very heavy chunks of ice. This ice will come in all sizes, even the smallest chunks of ice will be very heavy. They will come in all shapes, sizes, and weights. It will not be like snow falling on the ground that you can see several 100 feet up in the air. These are killer particles of ice that will fall very rapidly day and night. They will come from all directions… over you, at you, in front of you, and from behind you. These chunks of ice will come so rapidly, that you will not be able to get out of the way. You will not see them until they are right upon you. You won't have time to move out of their path.

All those people who live and walk in the Lord Jesus Christ will not have to go through the heat or the ice mentioned in these two visions. This is serious business folks! Are you saying to yourself, "Well what shall I do before it's too late for me?" You have to take the first step. Jesus is waiting for you to take it now. You have to re-adjust your mindset and heart. Now! You have to mean this with all of your heart, soul, and mind for this to work for you. God sees and knows your heart. He knows if you really mean it or not.

Are you ready? Here we go. Say these words of prayer with me, "Dear Lord Jesus, please hear my humble prayer. Lord, I know I am a Sinner and I have sinned against you and your holy laws. Lord, I want to change all of this and the sinful life I have been living. I know that Jesus Christ died to save me, and I am asking you right now, Lord Jesus, please forgive me of all my sins. Please come into my heart. Please let me be reborn in your Holy Spirit. I mean this, Lord Jesus, very sincerely with all my heart. In Jesus's holy name I pray. Amen and Amen.

If you really meant this prayer with all your heart, Jesus will take care of the rest.

Here is one of God's promises for you: Jeremiah 24: 7, *"and I will give them a heart to know me, that I am the*

Lord, and you shall be my people and I will be your God:
if they will turn to me with their whole heart."

God the father provided his only son Jesus Christ to be the ultimate sacrifice for us. We can be assured that God will meet all of our needs in accordance with his will. We must not ask out of greed or selfishness if we want to see God answer our prayers. It's always best to put the needs of others first before our own. Remember, we want to have as much favor as we can in God's answer to our prayers. When you see something in the Bible that fits exactly your situation, that is the Bible reading you. Yes, the Bible reads us. This is the connection that God has allowed you to have with him.

Remember, God is all powerful.

NOVEMBER 14TH, 2017

Last night as I was asleep in my bed, I dreamed I was in this very large warehouse building. It was 150 to 200 feet tall. Many people were inside this building working as I was. At another time, in another building, I heard one trumpet sounding very loudly. I quickly looked around the building to see who else heard this trumpet sound. Suddenly, I was being lifted up towards the top ceiling of this building. I started floating and going out of the top of the roof. I traveled in this floating experience to New York City.

In another vision I was sitting on this ladder several 100 feet in the air. I fell off of the ladder from the top and started falling quickly to the ground. Then, about 50 feet from the ground, I started floating gently to the ground. You see we, in this earthly body, live in dimensions and limitations. It is hard for us to understand what the spiritual life is like unless God enlightens us and allows us to have these spiritual dreams and visions That bring us into these realities of the spiritual world.

All of God's children will be of and live in the spiritual world and this physical world will be a thing of the past. Will you be with us, or will you be staying behind in this world as it is?

In the spiritual world, there is such a thing called the rapture of the church. What is this? It will be the removal of all God's people from the earth in 11/1 hundredths of a second, before all hell breaks loose here on earth, before the tribulation period. This is what the Bible tells us. So, where you stand with God determines if you will be included in this great endeavor.

God's people are divided on when the rapture of the church will take place. Some believe it will be before all the tribulation begins here on the earth (pre-tribulation); some believe the rapture will be halfway into the tribulation period (3 ½ years or mid-tribulation); and some believe the rapture will occur at the end of the tribulation period (7 years or post-tribulation). The Bible does not say when. It does state that no one knows the day nor the hour, not even the Son, but only the Father. I want to go out in the first rapture. However, no matter when it occurs, I know that Jesus will take care of all of us who love Him until that time.

Let us take a look at a "what if" situation if the rapture takes place in the middle of the tribulation. The Bible tells us that there will be a great falling away of God's people from Him before the rapture of the church. This might be because the Antichrist is already on the location of the earth. He may be doing great and awesome wonders that the Bible tells us about, causing many to fall away from God who were once God's children.

Hopefully, at some point, God's people will see the charade of the Antichrist and begin to remember what they know the Bible says, and they will come back to the Lord Jesus Christ. In that time, I perceive there will be many reasons that people will choose to turn away from Jesus Christ. Will any of these come back?

Another reason people believe that we may have to go through the tribulation is because of all the suffering Jesus Christ went through at the hands of the religious leaders leading to his death on the cross. Also, all the suffering the apostles and prophets in both the Old and New Testaments went through. Much of this is my own opinion. Let's move on from this topic as there is more information I want to share with you.

September 14th, 2014

Sunday, after church, three of us were talking in the parking lot of the church and an amazing light display took place. Brilliantly and absolutely captivating, were these hundreds of blue and gold vibrant colors. It was so amazing; I was almost speechless. I said to the others who were standing with me, "Did you all see that!" "No, "no, we didn't see anything". I said to them, "I saw hundreds of dazzling bright blue and gold lights!"

Some weeks after that I was at work at my job in the oil refinery. I was walking out of the fabrication shop, which was a very large building some 200 feet long and about 100 feet tall. Coming out of this fab shop, I looked up and in the eastern skies, I saw hundreds and hundreds of balloons ascending up to heaven. They were every color in all different shades of colors. What an amazing sight that was. I'm so grateful and thankful that the Lord blessed me so greatly with a wealth of visions and dreams.

In concluding the chapters of this book, I want to share with you something of deadly importance. It's about evil forces and why they're here today. In my previous book, "The End has Already Passed... Why are You Still Here?", I wrote down Satan's fall from heaven: Isaiah 14:12-15. Today in this book, "How Do I Talk to God... How Do I Find Favor with God?", I put this at the end of this book because it is very important for you to know. It is a matter of your life and your death!

If you don't have a Bible, I'll write this out for you. This is his especially for you. Ezekiel 28:13-17. Remember, Satan was full of wisdom and beauty.

> "Thou hast been in Eden, the garden of God; Every precious stone was thy covering, they sardius, Topaz and the diamond, the beryl, the Onyx, and the Jasper, the sapphire, the emerald, big carbuncle, and gold. The workmanship of thy tabrets and of thy pipes was prepared in thee in the day that thou was created. Thou art the anointed cherub that covereth and I, God, have set these so; thou was upon the holy

mountain of God; Thou hast walked up and down in the midst of the stones of fire. Thou was perfect in all thy ways from the day that thou was created till iniquity was found in the period by the multitude of thy merchandise they have filled the midst of thee with violence and thou hast sinned. Therefore, I will cast thee as a profane out of the mountain of God and I will destroy thee oh covering cherub from the midst of the stones of the fire. Thy heart was lifted up because of thy great beauty. Thy has corrupted thy wisdom by reason of thy brightness. I will cast thee to the ground."

The reason that the above information is so important is because the invisible evil forces are all around us and you need to know that they are doing as much harm and evil to us as they possibly can. They are invisible folks, and you need to know this so you can decide where you will spend eternity, in heaven or hell.

I have tried to reveal to you how much all the evil forces hate us written in this book and also in my first book,

"The End has Already Past…Why are You Still Here?" I pray you will give very serious consideration to the words of both these two books and make Jesus Christ the Lord and Savior of your life.

Let's meet up in heaven.

Robert

NOTES